ALI SIDDIQ

DOMINO EFFECT

DOMINO EFFECT

Published in Houston, TX
by What's Funny! LLC

www.alisiddiq.com

Edited by Leah Pride
Cover Design by John V. Bruton
Photographer: David Wright

ISBN: 978-1-955622-09-7 (hardcover)
979-8-396972-76-6 (paperback)

PRINTED IN THE UNITED STATES OF AMERICA

In life, people make mistakes…

TABLE OF CONTENTS

FOREWORD

By Roland S. Martin

When B.B. King died, I interviewed a variety of luminaries about the King of Blues. One of them was Lionel Richie. Richie, a great singer and songwriter in his own right, told the story of talking to King while both were in Italy. B.B. told him, "Lionel, you can't write the blues sitting in the back of a limousine."

Great comedians don't just stand on stage and tell jokes. They allow their lived experience to come through them, and they are able to find humor in the good and bad of their lives. Ali Siddiq is one of those individuals.

There are times when you look at Ali and wonder, "Why is he so serious?" Then he starts smiling and lets out a laugh. But Ali's life hasn't been one of shits and giggles. He has experienced the lowest of the lows and the highest of the highs. Yet through it all, he has maintained a commitment to be true to himself. What is most needed today—from the pulpit to the comedy stage—are truth tellers willing to say what needs to be said, and critics be damned. Ali fits the bill. I knew Dick Gregory well, and he is certainly in the mold of Dick: a fierce social commentator on the world using the biting humor of the stage. Not everyone can pull this off with ease because it's not easy. It takes hard work, a commitment to the craft, and a willingness to be open and vulnerable.

We all should be thankful that in this day and age, Ali Siddiq is one of the few comics who brings a no-holds-barred persona to the stage, all the while keeping us laughing and wanting more.

INTRODUCTION

For every action, there's a reaction. For every cause, there's an effect. Some people call it Newton's law, causation, karma, or simply reaping what you've sown. In my comedy special, I called it the "domino effect." Now, I'm not talking about the game you and your homeboys play at the barbeque. I'm talking about how one event in your life can trigger a series of events, and before you know it, you're manifesting a destiny you've never dreamed of. This could be a good thing or a bad thing. It could have a positive outcome or a negative one. This could work in your favor or totally against you, but ultimately, you control how the pendulum swings. What you can't control is what causes the dominoes to begin falling in your life or when the effect will end.

I've seen extravagant and elaborate displays with thousands, even millions, of dominoes. The dominoes are intentionally set up to fall in a coordinated, strategic fashion to carve out the image of a person, picture, or phrase. Every single domino has a part to play in the design. How and when they fall is essential in the mind of their creator. Whether we know it or not, our lives are set up just like dominoes. The events in our lives are connected and crash into each other, painting an unedited portrait of us that defines who we are. Whether the events are good, bad, happy, tragic, or triumphant doesn't matter. The only thing that matters is that they are real and critical to how we function in life.

The messed-up thing about the whole domino effect situation is that you are not usually the one who knocks down the first domino in your life. The person who triggers the domino avalanche in your life is usually a parent or relative. Unfortunately, things your parents say and do can have a lasting negative impact on you. I know your mind went straight to rape, molestation, or some other form of abuse, but words can be just as powerful and much more destructive.

Once again, I'm not talking about a parent cursing you out, saying, "You ain't shit," or, "You're gonna be just like yo' no-good daddy…" (nothing harsh and intentional like that). Most of the time, it's the unintentional parental mistakes that make the biggest impact and deepest scars. For example, when parents use fear, intimidation, and threats to keep their kids in line, but instead it makes them timid and scared to express themselves, or when a parent overreacts to every situation, crippling the child emotionally and causing them to grow up not knowing how to manage disappointments in life.

The most common mistake I've seen parents make is living vicariously through their kids and micromanaging their lives, trying to get them to avoid the same mistakes they made and accomplish the dreams and goals they couldn't. In this case, the child can't wait to get the hell away from their parents. Often, they end up making poor decisions that could have been avoided had the parents created an environment conducive to their independence, growth, and individuality.

I could easily blame my parents for the shit show that happened in my life. My mother was a single parent trying to raise three kids. She made mistakes trying to provide for and protect us the best way she could. My father was both absent and present during stages of my life, so I could surely blame my issues on his inconsistencies and the criminal behavior he exposed me to. Instead, I'll just blame myself—mainly because I know the exact moment I fucked up and kicked down my first domino. It doesn't matter what dominoes my parents knocked down beforehand. I know what I did, and I own that.

My domino effect started when I was ten. Yeah, it didn't take me long to end up on the wrong damn road. One emotional decision at a tender age charted a course that would ultimately land me in prison ten years later. I was young, dumb, and unsatisfied with the life I had. Ungrateful for my blessings, I decided I wanted something different. Ain't that the way it always happens? The grass always looks greener on the other side until you get there and realize that maybe you should have just watered your own damn grass.

We all have moments in our lives when we feel insignificant or our efforts go unnoticed. These are the times we go searching for affirmation and applause from strangers instead of appreciating the soldiers in our own camp. This is dangerous because our need for attention causes us to make poor decisions, and the dominoes start to fall in the wrong direction—mine certainly did. My mother was crazy, but she was my ride-or-die. She had my back, my front, and my backside if I ever tried her, which is why I never did. Well, at least not in front of her face.

So, I was ten, and my father had been MIA for seven years. Suddenly, he decided he wanted to be a daddy and take care of his kids. Without hesitation, my dumb ass volunteered to go live with a maniac. Undoubtedly, this was the start of my demise, but I will expound more about that fiasco later in the book. I just wanted you to know that I knew when and where it all started, and I take full responsibility for my mistake. I also know that most people wouldn't take responsibility. They'd blame everything on everyone else and never come to grips with the fact that they just made a bad decision. We have all made bad decisions. It's a very common and inevitable part of life. It has been said, "If it doesn't kill you, it makes you stronger." If you are reading this book, you're not dead, and you've been given another chance to get it right.

Expert domino toppers and builders use a technique called the "safety gap." When you are setting up a domino display with thousands of dominoes, you remove at least five dominoes to create safety gaps throughout the display just in case you trigger a collapse prematurely. The safety gap stops the progression so you can reset and redirect the dominoes. It's my sincere hope that you will allow this book to serve as a safety gap in your life. If things are falling apart or moving in the wrong direction, please use my poor choices, character flaws, wild stories, and encounters with criminals, crackheads, and convicts to help you redirect some things!

I'm giving you permission to look at my shit, laugh at my shit, and most importantly, learn from my shit so you can run like hell when that shit shows up in your life. When I was in it, I had no clue that there was a reset button, nor did I know I had the power to press it. I've had to press that button a thousand times. I'll probably have to press it a thousand more times, but the blessing is in simply knowing that it's there. I hate starting over, but I will gladly do it, especially if it helps me maintain my sanity, defines my destiny, and keeps me out of prison.

Alright, now let's get back to my daddy and that dumb-ass decision I made in 1983...

"There go yo' daddy."

CHAPTER 1

1983

I don't mean to brag, but I consider myself extremely blessed to have grown up during the '70s and '80s. It was truly one of the greatest times to be alive, especially for Black people. We were smoking weed with the white folks at Woodstock, wearing afros and platform shoes, and driving Cadillacs. Muhammad Ali was knocking niggas out, Kareem was balling, and we were starring in movies like *Shaft* and *Cooley High* and TV shows like *Good Times*, *What's Happening!!*, and *The Jeffersons*.

Let us not forget some of the best music the world has ever heard was made during the '70s and '80s. Black Power and Black Pride were on full display, and it was a beautiful thing.

I personally was having the time of my life being wild and free, roaming the neighborhoods, climbing trees, riding bicycles, playing hide-and-seek, eating cool cups, snacking on summer sausage, and staying outside until the streetlights came on. During the weekdays, I went to school and played basketball in the park with my friends. But Saturdays were my absolute favorite. I'd wake up early, get a big bowl of cereal, and watch my favorite cartoons, *Fat Albert* and *Super Friends.*

My mother would make us clean the house from top to bottom. Erica, my older sister, would wash the dishes and dust the furniture. Mom would do the laundry and fold clothes. I would take care of the floors, since mopping and vacuuming were my specialties. It was hard work, but I didn't mind because my mother would crank up the music and play classics like the O'Jays; Stevie Wonder; Gladys Knight; Chaka Khan; Earth, Wind & Fire; Frankie Beverly and Maze; and the Jackson Five.

I used to pretend I was live in concert, sliding all over the floor with the mop as my microphone and Erica as my audience. She'd gas me up as I made a complete fool of myself. We'd finish cleaning just in time to watch kung fu movies and *Soul Train*. Afterward, I'd catch up with my friends and we'd go roam the neighborhoods, making peace and war with the kids on the block.

Those were the days. I wouldn't trade them for anything in the world. Life was so simple back then. No flossing or fronting, no social media, political correctness, or pop or cancel culture, and no one judged you by the clothes you wore, the car you drove, or the house you lived in. Everything was so chill because we were all the same. Everybody was trying to make ends meet, but we were all content and grateful for the little that we had.

At that moment in time, African Americans had endured so much. From slavery to civil rights, segregation to integration, and the assassinations of our leaders to the enforcement of systemic racism. All of those negative dominoes were crashing and falling around us at the same time, but somehow, we still found the strength to rise and shine. It's been said that light shines brightest in darkness. Some of the greatest musical geniuses of all time emerged during the '70s and '80s, artists like Stevie Wonder, Aretha Franklin, Michael Jackson, Prince, and Whitney Houston, to name a few. This only proves our resilience as a people and our ability to make the best out of unfortunate situations.

The domino effect can only be effective if it affects our will to rise above.

In the early '70s, my parents split, so my mother was raising my sister and me alone. I was very young when my father left the house, so my memories of him are vague. I knew who he was because he used to pop up randomly at different locations, and my mother would be like, "There go yo' daddy." He was always fun whenever I saw him, so my overall impression of him was pleasant.

My mom later got a live-in boyfriend, but my impression of him was the complete opposite.

Hate is such a strong word. But, in this case, it's fair to say I hated this dude. I was just a kid, but I knew something about him just rubbed me the wrong way. Maybe it was because he was mean as nails and both verbally and physically abusive. Yep, I'm pretty sure that was the reason. I rarely questioned my mother's judgment, but I often wondered why she subjected herself and her kids to an asshole like that. Her reasoning could have been financially motivated, since she was now a single parent. Despite that, it was awkward having him in the house because it no longer felt like a home with him there.

One day he got beside himself, crossed the line, and put his hands on me—not as an adult would discipline a child, but more like a coward would victimize someone he knew couldn't defend themselves. Without question, that started a domino effect in my life. It caused me to develop a serious complex about people putting their hands on me or touching me without my permission.

I've gotten into plenty of fights and even spent a few nights in jail due to the trauma and anger that was triggered in me by this man. Though the negative effects of my abuser have hung over my head, I have decided I won't allow them to control my life, my actions, or my reactions. It took me some time to get here. I still have a long way to go, but I just wanted you to know that no matter what has happened to you, you still have the power to control your own narrative and destiny.

Shortly after the incident he and I had, my mother decided to leave him. Whatever financial stability he provided for us did not compensate for the threat he had become to our family and our life. Erica and I were relieved that he was gone, but suddenly, in a whirlwind, we relocated to Mississippi. My mother told us she needed some time to get her life together and that she was sending my sister and me away to live with my family in Mississippi. My mother has always been responsible, and one characteristic of being responsible is knowing when to hit the reset button.

In our family, when someone sends out a distress signal, we always respond with open arms and open doors. I can honestly say we all have lived with a family member at some point in our lives, especially if the goal was the betterment of ourselves or our situation. This was the case for my mother. She wanted to make something of her life. She was young and still had time to turn the tide, so she made a very precise and sacrificial move to advance. My mother understood that her dominoes were falling in the wrong direction. Extracting us from the situation was necessary to change the course of her life and ours. I didn't understand it at the time, but I do now. My mom knew we'd be in good hands and that her family would take very good care of us in Mississippi.

I equate living with my family in Mississippi to that thick, colorful crochet blanket that Grandma used to make. It may have been itchy, ugly, and heavy, but it kept you warm and comfy when it was cold outside. While living in Mississippi, I was fed, clothed, housed, and safe. At the end of the day, that's all that mattered to my mother.

Mississippi was very different from Houston. If you've never been to the Deep South, it's everything you thought it would be but slower, poorer, and way more country. I'm talking dirt roads, rednecks, roadkill, farmhouses, and rolling hills kind of country. You didn't have the option of playing outside till the streetlights came on because there were none. If you got caught in the dark in Mississippi, you were just lost until the sun came up. You'd better pray the Ku Klux Klan wasn't marching that night.

My grandmother was strict, stern, and structured just like my mother. That's why I opted to live with my aunt Angela, who was much more carefree. While with my aunt Angela, we lived in both Mississippi and Chicago. We had family in both places.

Chicago was nice because it gave me a much-needed break from Mississippi. It felt like I had stepped out of a time capsule and back into civilization. Though Chicago was a big city, it was different from Houston. The buildings were taller, the pace was faster, and the weather was cold as hell! Despite the freezing weather, it was nice to get to know a side of my family I had never met before. We lived in Chicago for almost a year, and then my aunt Angela decided to move back to Mississippi.

All the moving around made me feel a type of way and amplified the fact that I really missed my mother. She would come visit us often and let us know how things were going. My mother was working multiple jobs and going to school, trying to obtain a degree in education. I knew she would accomplish her goal because she was so purpose-driven and focused. Building a career for herself and a better life for her kids was her main priority. Though I missed seeing her face every day, I was very proud of my mother. She would assure us that this was only temporary and we'd be back with her soon.

So it was 1983, Michael Jackson dropped "Billie Jean," and the world went crazy, especially in the Black community. We'd seen niggas do a lot of shit, but we ain't never seen a nigga glide backward before. That move put Michael Jackson right up there with Jesus in our eyes. On a random day in Mississippi, I was in the front yard practicing the moonwalk, and my aunt Angela pulled up. Just like that, she told Erica and me to pack our bags because we were moving back to Houston. I thought she was playing, but she wasn't. It was true, my mother had officially sent for us, and we were going home!

My mother had done exactly what she said she would do…

She finished college, got a teaching job and a new apartment, and was ready for her kids to be back with her in H-Town! I'm not going to lie; I couldn't have been happier! I loved being in the city. I enjoy the fast pace, the noisy neighbors, the police sirens, and even the pollution. Plus, I couldn't wait to reconnect with my friends!

Life was good. I was back in the H, and everything was lovely except for this little big problem. My mother was pregnant, and she had a new boyfriend. Red flags and flashbacks of the terrorist she was with before hit me like a ton of bricks. I immediately put up my guard, ignoring the fact that he really was different. He was quiet, reserved, and seemed like a nice guy, but I didn't care. I wanted no part of him, and there was nothing anyone could say to make me change my mind.

It wasn't long before the baby came, and soon we had a baby sister. She was so beautiful... yet very noisy at the same damn time. I couldn't believe such a tiny person could cry so loud and so often. I shared a room with my older sister. I didn't mind because we had bunk beds and I could fly off the top bunk like Superman anytime I wanted. Our apartment was much bigger than before and so much nicer. It was plain to see that our living situation had improved.

My only problem was I was living in the house with three women...

When I lived with my aunt Angela, I at least had my boy cousins to bond with, but now, I had no one or nothing I could relate to. Everything was soft, delicate, dainty, and fragrant. I couldn't find unscented toiletries nowhere in the goddamn house! Do you know how embarrassing it is to walk into the school smelling like Dove soap and Johnson & Johnson's baby lotion?

Not to mention, my sister was twelve, so her hormones and emotions were all over the place, my mother was post-partum, so she was either yelling at us or crying, and the baby was an uncontrollable narcissist, demanding all the attention in the house.

Basically, I was in female estrogen hell! Not a sign of toxic masculinity anywhere except for the new boyfriend, and I wasn't feeling him at all.

Then one day, it happened. My get-out-of-jail-free card knocked at the door.

My silly ass yelled, “Who is it?”

A deep, dark voice from the other side of the door said, “It’s your daddy.”

I was like, “Oh shit!”

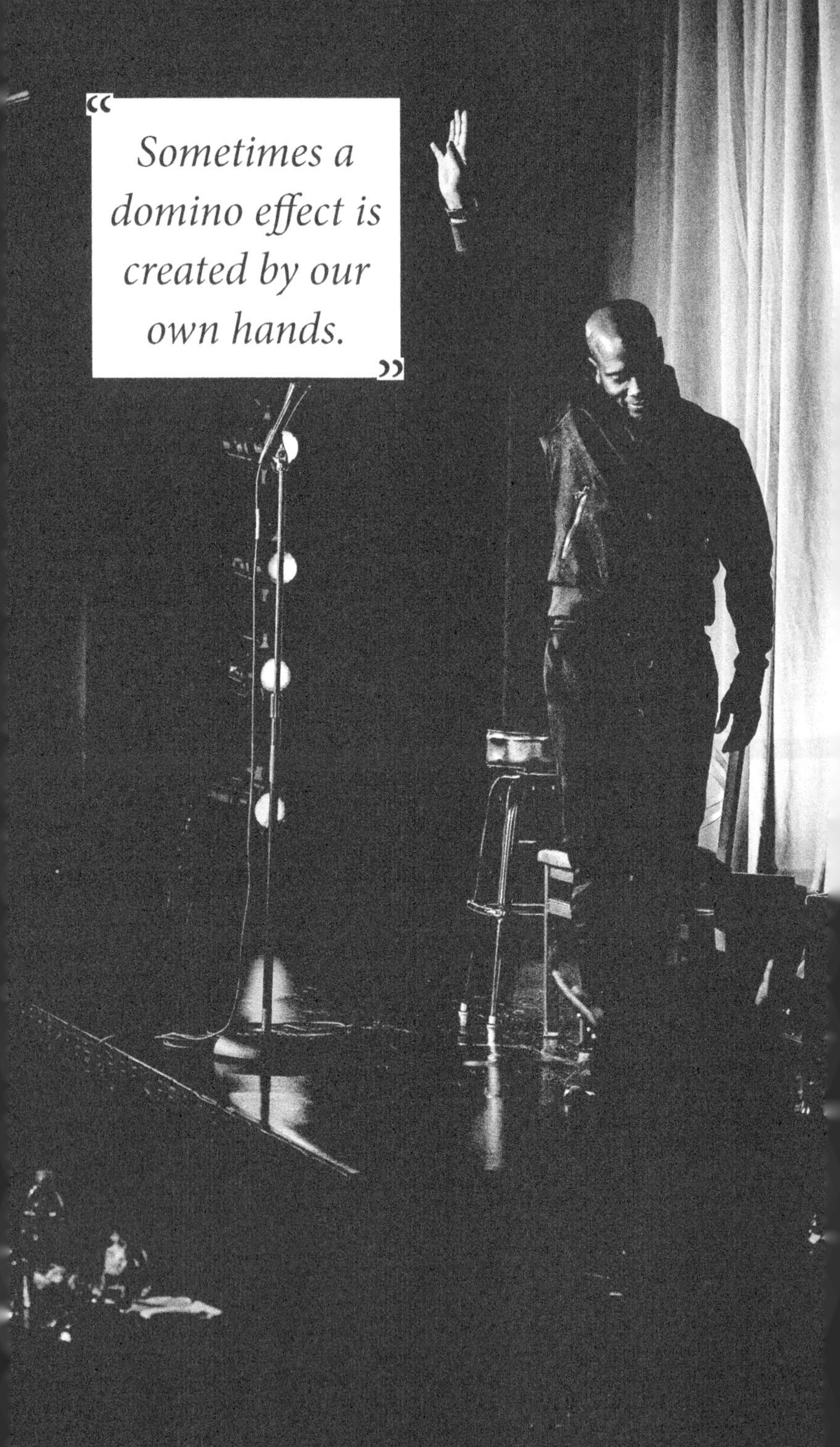
"Sometimes a domino effect is created by our own hands."

CHAPTER 2

WHAT Y'ALL WANNA DO?

They say when opportunity knocks, you must answer the door. Well, opportunity came to my door in the form of my biological father. The wind literally blew his ass in. He either heard or had gotten wind that we were back in town, and he came to see us.

He came into my mother's apartment and greeted us with hugs, tickles, and some weird random questions that neither myself nor my sister knew how to answer. After a few moments of awkward silence and giggles, my mother dismissed us so she and my father could talk. In a nutshell, my father came to talk to my mother about having his kids come to live with him.

I knew this because I decided to be nosey and ear hustle instead of going to my room like my mother told me.

Now, here lies the problem. As previously mentioned, my dad left when I was just three years old. I was now ten. It'd been seven years since I'd lived with my father, so he was basically a stranger to me. I'd seen him every blue moon, and that was usually by accident.

We did not have any arranged visits with him every other weekend. He didn't have us on alternating holidays like Thanksgiving or Christmas, nothing like that. Not to mention, he didn't come to visit us in Mississippi at all.

So I was confused as to why he believed me or my sister was going to stay with him after these brief random interactions. In his defense, every time I'd seen him, he'd been fun, but so was going to McDonald's. Just because Ronald McDonald was fun didn't mean I should go live with him.

To my knowledge, my father hadn't been a full-time parent ever, so how did he think he even qualified? What made him want to sign up for daddy duty in the first place? Was he watching *Good Times* and had a James Evans moment? Did he read a parenting magazine and get a wild idea? It all seemed very weird to me, but I admired his ambition. In fact, his ambition became my inspiration, but not in a good way.

Let me explain…

In my ten-year-old mind, I began to ponder how I could make my father's unforeseen interest in his kids work to my advantage. First off, all this girly stuff in the house was getting on my damn nerves. I felt like I was trapped in the land of sugar and spice and everything nice.

Secondly, I couldn't stand the "boyfriend." Every time I saw him, I wanted to punch him in the face! If he ever thought about putting his hands on me like the last boyfriend, I was going to snap. So my current situation was okay, but it could've been better. Having said that, I felt I'd be doing myself a huge disservice if I didn't properly weigh my options.

To be honest, I didn't know my father, but he seemed cool. He was a handsome guy. He was dressed fresh. His shoes were shined. He wore a nice watch, and he drove a Lincoln. I mean, I could actually learn to like this guy. He had style; he had swag, and most importantly, he was manly. I'm pretty sure he had unscented lotion in his crib too, which was a plus, but I was still torn.

Just out of curiosity, I wanted to know more about the man standing in my living room, whom I was the spitting image of. Would being around him give me clues as to who I was or the man I'd eventually become? Was I more like him? Was I more like his daddy, or maybe one of his brothers whom I had never met? Questions, questions, questions. I didn't know the answers, but I was curious. They say curiosity killed the cat, but how exactly did the cat die? Did he die because he was curious? Or did he die because he got hit by a bus chasing a mouse?

In 1983, there was no Ancestory.com, so if I wanted to know more about my roots, my father was the gateway. All of these thoughts were going through my mind as I eavesdropped.

Then, out of nowhere, I got hit with a curve ball…My mama said, "Okay."

What the hell! What was she doing? We just got back, and she was trying to give us away again! My mom had to be playing chicken with him.

Maybe she was thinking, "Ain't no way my children are going to willingly go stay with Mr. Stranger Danger." Or maybe she was just tired of us? I really didn't know!

I was confused by all of this. I ran back into the room, looking like I had just seen a ghost. Before my sister could ask what was wrong, my mother walked into our room and said, "Sit down, we need to talk."

She went on to explain my father's proposition. Then she hit us with another curve ball. She said, "So what y'all want to do?"

Well I be damned!

First of all, you're not supposed to ask your children what they want to do. We don't have enough cognitive intervention skills to make a rational decision. All I knew was my dad was fun when I saw him every blue moon. That's it! Secondly, my mama had never cared about what we wanted to do before, so I was wondering why this lady was asking us this. I raise my children the same way my mom raised me. I don't ask my kids what they want to eat, ever. I put food down in front of them like wild animals: "There it is." It's on them if they eat it or not. I've done my part. It's not my decision no more.

The decision my mother had set before my sister and me that day was way more important than food. It felt like we were suddenly transported into a game of double jeopardy. The decision was easy for Erica, but for me, it was difficult. This was my father, and I was his son. That's an important relationship in a man's life. Unlike many Black fathers, he wanted me in his life and in his house. I was at a crossroads. This was a defining moment for me that could change my life forever. Did I want to spend my life wondering what could have been, or know what it was?

With my mother's permission, my dad entered our bedroom for the moment of truth: "Do you want to leave with me or stay with your mother?" was the question he proposed. My sister's face was like, "Shiiid!" She took two steps back and said, "Nah, I'm cool!" I'm pretty sure my mother was thinking, I was gonna say the same thing, but she was sadly mistaken.

"Yes, I'll leave with you," I said. The entire room was shook!

My mother, my sister, and even my daddy were in shock, but I wasn't. Deep inside, I was ready to turn over a new leaf, swim in uncharted waters, and take a walk on the wild side. My daddy was fun, friendly, and fresh. That was good enough for me.

The smart thing to do was to follow my sister's lead, but I wasn't that smart. I was only ten years old. Erica was two years older than me. She'd known my father longer; thus, she had more information. I'm pretty sure that was the basis for her decision, but my decision was based solely on his presentation. Looking back, I should have listened to Erica, because she definitely tried to warn me.

I was in the room packing my shit, and Erica was giving me the eyes. She was like, "Are you sure? You know, Mama's house has a lot of amenities."

What she was really trying to say was, our house was set up for kids. We had food, snacks, running water, electricity, and necessary shit like that. My mother was a planner, and she had thoroughly prepared for us to live, function, and be safe at her house. She provided everything we needed in one place.

Sometimes we can't see the forest for the trees. We're so blinded by what we want instead of focusing on what we need. That's what I did. I was young and made an innocent mistake, not knowing that life can come at you hard and it doesn't care about your age or your innocence.

The cruelest thing about the domino effect is that it's no respecter of person, age, race, nationality, creed, or time of day. At any given moment, someone or something could knock a domino down and cause your whole life to implode. You can lose a loved one or your job, get into an accident, get divorced, or be the victim of a natural disaster, violent crime, or vicious attack.

It's never a question of *if* any of these things will happen; it's always a question of *when.* How you respond when it happens defines who you are, and that can be an eye-opener. Most of us don't really know what's in us until we've been tried, tested, and proven.

Unfortunately, many of us are born into a domino effect situation and have to fight the rest of our lives to stop the progression. I can't control the fact that I was born a Black male or that I spent the majority of my life in a single-parent home. I had no clue that the schools I went to were under-educating me and not effectively preparing me for success in life.

Many people don't understand that religion has crippled them or that tradition has crushed their ability to think freely. Systemic racism, welfare reform, discrimination, and police brutality were realities before I was born. I had to live through poverty, political corruption, and the crack epidemic of the '80s; these were all domino effects that I didn't create but had to manage.

Sometimes a domino effect is created by our own hands. Our ambitions, wants, needs, hopes, and dreams can cause us to make irrational, desperate decisions that contribute to our own demise. My desire to get to know a man who had already abandoned me for seven years stirred emotions, created experiences, and exposed me to things I would have been protected from had I made a wise decision.

They say that experience is the best teacher... but that's bullshit. Wisdom is the best teacher. Your own experiences are not the only way you can get wisdom. You can watch how others stick and move, rise and fall, and become wiser. Learning how to walk, talk, and move wisely in life is critical. Unfortunately, I had to learn this the hard way, but you don't.

> *"Every day was like boot camp, and my mother was the drill sergeant!"*

CHAPTER 3

NO FUN

"Black excellence" is a term often used in today's society, but this is nothing new to me. I saw it every day in the life of my mother. My mother embodied the essence of excellence. Her work ethic, how she carried herself, how she governed her house, and how she raised her kids were a direct reflection of the type of quality woman she was. You would have thought my mother had a military background the way she had Erica and me marching around that house like soldiers. Every day was like boot camp, and my mother was the drill sergeant, grilling the hell out of us. She cooked my ass all the time because I was always doing something I had no business doing. I was just being a kid, but my mother wasn't trying to hear that.

She was in a delicate situation, being a single mother. The road was tougher, and the stakes were higher. We literally couldn't afford to make a mistake because mistakes would slow down the process and progression of our family. For example, getting in trouble at school meant my mother would have to take off work. Missing a day of work means missing a day of pay. This would result in her not having enough money to pay bills at the end of the month. If we messed up, it could literally result in us being homeless.

My mother used to constantly remind us that she didn't have time for incidents, accidents, or tragedies. My mom was like, "Be where you're supposed to be. Do what you're supposed to do. If it looks like it's about to be trouble, come your ass home."

My mother was stern, structured, and extremely organized. If something was out of place, she would notice immediately because she kept everything in order. When company came over, she never had to say, "Excuse the house," because her house was always immaculate. Though we were poor, it didn't feel like it. My mother would work her "Black girl magic" and manage to make a dollar out of fifteen cents every single time. Like most little Black boys, I thought my mother was crazy and way too serious. I guess that's why I became a comedian, because I was always trying to make her laugh so she could loosen up.

My mother was like a joke with no punch line. Sex with no orgasm. A brand-new car with no steering column. As much as you wanted to enjoy her, you couldn't because she was no fun! I often wonder how she and my dad got together because he was a circus and she was a cemetery. Maybe she was fun when she was younger and having kids sucked all the fun out of her and turned her into Major Payne. Of course, all of this changed as we became adults and were able to take care of ourselves. But when we were kids, she played no games…literally.

My mama had a lot of rules, and everything was a matter of life or death. Even things that were supposed to be fun, like going outside, she'd turn into a Lifetime movie. I remember my mama called me and my sister into the room and said, "Hey, I need to talk to y'all right now. Are y'all listening to me? This is a matter of *life* and *death*. I'ma give you a key to the front door. You put that key on your neck, and you don't let nobody know you have this key because they will *kill* you."

Keep in mind, I was only seven years old. She put the key around my neck, and I felt like I'd just been given the five Infinity Stones and the fate of the entire universe was upon me. So I was outside playing, and I noticed the goddamn key wasn't around my neck.

My first thought was, "I'm going to die! I don't want to die! I've got to find my key." I panicked! I was so nervous. I started crying and walking around the apartment complex, searching desperately for my key and my sister, Erica.

With tears and snot streaming down my face, I asked a stranger, "Hey, man, you seen my sister?"

Erica saw me from a distance. She already knew what was wrong. She said, "Boy, where your key at?" I just broke down because I knew either my mama was going to kill me or *they* were going to kill me. Whoever *they* was.

I've been scared of *they* all my damn life. This is completely my mother's fault. She was always telling us what "they" said or what "they" gone do.

"*They* gone get you." "*They* gone block you." "*They* gone take you." "*They* gone get you in trouble." "*They* said the weather's gone be bad"...

Your mother ever told you where not to be? My mama would be like, "Don't go over there." And you went over there anyway and got hurt. You couldn't call for help because you were not supposed to be over there. Now you had to bear crawl your way to a neutral place just to receive aid. Your arm and your leg were broken, but you were more traumatized by your mother finding out where you were than the pain.

I couldn't even go outside without her giving me a lecture. She'd say, "Hey, if you're going outside, don't be like them badass little boys and go to that pool. The pool is closed. Don't jump that damn gate and be over there by the damn pool." I was outside for fifteen minutes, and everybody else had jumped that gate. My goofy ass jumped right over the gate too. Now, you know something was going to happen because kids are bad as hell.

A few moments later, I got pushed into the pool. I hadn't had a swimming lesson in my life. Somehow, my mama knew I was in that pool. You know mothers have women's intuition. My mama just heard the splash and came outside. I saw my mama as I was going down. You know, I swam underwater to the other side of the pool and got out of the water. By the time my mama got to me, I was out of that pool. She told me, "Your ass better been out that goddamn water by the time I got to you, or I was going to beat your ass while you were drowning."

My mama was no fun, but she was funny as hell. In so many ways, I'm just like my mother. I govern my house the exact same way she did. I don't like things out of place or out of order. I don't function well in chaotic situations.

Chaos, clutter, and confusion are breeding grounds for failure.

Organization, precision, and diligence are the breeding grounds for success.

I joke a lot about my mother, but she was the one who put me up on game about the domino effect. She was like a coach sharing all the information she knew, so I could win this game called life. She understood that, like dominoes, mistakes can crash into each other, forming patterns, habits, and cycles that are very hard to break.

Black men are potentially at risk. There are traps and systems intentionally set up for us to ruin our lives. I believe my mother knew this early on and was trying to save me. She was no fun because she took parenting seriously. I commend her for being such an amazingly responsible mother. I'll always love her for that.

"...canned rice, Fiesta shoes, and loaded baked potatoes..."

CHAPTER 4

CRABS

My father was born and raised in Louisiana. He was the second oldest of eight children and the only man I've ever called Father. I count it a privilege and an honor to have known my father.

I understand that many Black males are not afforded this opportunity. Though I am grateful for our relationship, I must admit it didn't start off on the best of terms. His seven-year disappearing act took a toll on me and created a chip on my shoulder.

In other words, a domino effect was started in my life that was rooted in rejection. Some might argue that I was young, and seven years is too short of a time span to create an impact, but I beg to differ. Tell that to someone doing a seven-year prison sentence or dealing with an illness for seven years. It's a long time because we only get twelve years of childhood, and my father was absent for most of mine.

Experts say the first seven years of a child's life are the most critical. Childhood is the period of receiving. Children receive the love and tenderness of their parents during this phase. This love will help them become good adults. Being that both my father and mother took breaks away from me during important years of my life hurt me. It has been said that time heals all wounds. The time I spent living with my dad initiated my healing process, and it all started in a grocery store called Fiesta.

I said my goodbyes to my mother and sister and left to start a new life with my father. It was actually more like an adventure, but I digress. On the way to his house, we stopped at Fiesta. For those of you who are not from the Houston area, Fiesta is like a carnival where groceries are sold. You can buy almost anything at Fiesta, from watches to wings, pork chops to patio furniture, and chitterlings to chia pets. You can even get your phone repaired, pay your light bill, and get your lashes done, all at the same store.

So we were at Fiesta picking up a few things and ended up in the seafood section. My dad noticed me looking hard at the crabs. He said, "You want some of them, crabs, boy?" I did, but I didn't know how to respond because this was not my first time seeing those crabs.

I'd been in that store before and seen those same crabs with my mother, but it was a very traumatizing experience. Remember, everything with my mama was either life or death. When I was looking at those crabs with her, she said, "Boy, you want some of them crabs?"

I said, "Yeah."

My mama looked at me and said, "Boy, do you want to eat for a day, or do you want to eat for a month?" Those crabs were $5.99 a pound—and I didn't know our financial situation!

My daddy was different. He didn't take life so seriously. He was fun, less calculated, and lived in the moment. He asked me again, "You want some of them crabs?"

Confused about what the correct response was, I said, "Maybe."

He said, "You can have the crabs, shit. My man, let me get fifteen pounds of them crabs."

In my mind, I was like, "Fifteen pounds! We ain't never eatin' again!"

We went home, and I experienced my first crab boil. My father boiled the crabs with potatoes and sausage. We ate and had an amazing time playing music, laughing, and talking. I was thinking, "If this is what it's going to be like living with my daddy, I made the right decision." I could not have been more wrong.

See, my daddy was carefree. In other words, he didn't care. I could go outside and just live my life. If something happened to me or I was abducted, it just happened. My father didn't micromanage me like my mother; he just let me run wild. If I lost a limb in the process—so be it. I'd just have to roll with the punches and accept it as a part of life.

My father was a bachelor, and in so many ways, he just was not prepared to be a parent. First of all, he lived in an all-adult apartment, so I was the only child in the entire complex. Not only was I living there illegally, but I was also exposed to all sorts of adult activities that my little eyes were not supposed to see.

Second, I had no one to play with, so most of the time I was bored and lonely. I had to travel a distance just to be around other kids. I finally made a friend named Julio that lived two apartment complexes down. When Julio was not around, I used to wander around different apartment complexes trying to find friends, which was dangerous.

Lastly, my father's house was just not set up for kids. From the rug on the wall of the naked lady to the joints in the candy dish on the living room table, it just was not an atmosphere conducive for kids to be in.

My living conditions were not deplorable, just not ideal. He converted his weight room into my bedroom. His weight bench and workout equipment were still in the room. He just threw a bed in the middle of the floor and was like, "There you go!" Let's just say getting up to go to the bathroom in the middle of the night was dangerous and potentially harmful.

The thing I missed the most about living with my mother was the food. My mama always had a pantry full of groceries because she was a quality woman and a qualified parent.

My dad—hmm, not so much. Moving in with him showed me the difference in parenting skills very fast. Kids can pick up on things. They know when they're in a safe environment and when the environment is hostile. It didn't take me long to realize I was living with a maniac.

In my mother's pantry, there were quality canned goods. The canned goods would have a picture of what was in the can and a company on the can that was responsible for what was in the can.

My daddy's pantry had cans with black-and-white labels with words on them, like "Corn," "Peas," and "Rice"!

I know you're saying, "In a can? Is the rice cooked? What kind of rice is in a can?" I asked the same questions, trust me.

What pissed me off was my daddy never knew what kind of corn was in the cans. There are different types of corn: creamed corn, whole corn, and sweet corn.

I'd be like, "Daddy, what kind of corn is it?"

He'd say, "I don't know. We're both going to be surprised."

My mom had quality groceries. My dad had quantity—in other words, a whole lot of shit I didn't want to eat.

The difference that stood out to me like a sore thumb was that my mother really knew me. She always bought exactly what I liked. When you're a kid, it's only a couple of things that are important to you: good cereal for breakfast and nice sneakers for your feet. That's it.

My mother would buy cereal that had a commercial and some representation or a mascot, like Sugar Smacks. Remember Sugar Smacks had that cool-ass bear walking around like he was trying to sell you heroin?

"Hey, you want some Sugar Smacks?" Fruit Loops had Toucan Sam flying around. "Who wants some Fruit Loops?" Those are the types of cereals my mother would buy us.

My dad would buy this shit called Fruity O's. When you're a kid, you're supposed to pour cereal out of a box. This shit came in a big-ass potato sack. You ain't supposed to take a bowl and scoop no goddamn cereal out of a bag like chicken feed.

I had to stand in front of the refrigerator with this big-ass bowl of scooped cereal and be like, "Dad, there ain't no milk."

He'd say, "The milk is in the cabinet."

"In the cabinet!"

"Yeah, you have to add water."

Add water…to milk? Man, it was poverty at its finest. I used to always wonder why my daddy would be in the kitchen talking about, "Hey, it's almost ready," shaking something.

What the hell do you mean, it's almost ready? Milk is supposed to already be ready, sir!

My mother would buy us name-brand sneakers so we'd have good-quality shoes for school. My daddy would just buy shit that he saw in the grocery store. He'd just roll through the grocery store and see some shoes, and he'd be like, "Man, try those shoes on."

"I don't want those shoes. The shoes are hanging by the bread, Dad. Why would I want shoes that are hanging by the bread?"

My daddy would make me try on them shoes. You know grocery store shoes are tied together with some hard-ass plastic contraption.

He would be like, "Man, turn around. Let me see."

I'd say, "I can't turn around. My feet are shackled together!"

To this day, I don't even know how my parents met, because they're two totally different people. They say that opposites attract, but, damn. Those two could be the poster children for night and day. They did have a few similarities: they both loved to dance, kept a clean house, and cared a lot about their appearance.

My father was always dressed fresh. His wardrobe was impeccable. He had about sixty black tailored suits, a hundred white shirts, a collection of black belts, and three types of shoes: boots, loafers, and lace-ups.

Ironically, my dad only owned two pairs of jeans, no shorts, and no ties. He said he was never gonna wear a noose around his neck. Though my father's parenting style was questionable, his overall style and fashion were on point.

People think I'm being hard on my father, but I'm not. I'm just convinced that he was not ready to be a parent. I don't know why he came over there playing with me like that.

Both my mother and I were trying to give him the benefit of the doubt, hoping someway, somehow, things would work themselves out, but they didn't. It just got progressively worse.

The most noticeable change that happened to me while under my father's care was my weight gain. I went from a size slim to a husky in a matter of months. It wasn't because I was eating good; it was the exact opposite.

Let me explain…

The average person eats a loaded baked potato a few times per year. I was eating a loaded baked potato about four times a day, for breakfast, lunch, dinner, and a snack. I was over the Fruity O's with powdered milk situation, so a loaded baked potato with no steak was the closest thing to normal I could find, and I just ran with it.

My dad didn't help. When he found out I liked baked potatoes, he kept feeding them to me like cattle. I was fully supplied with a ten-pound sack of potatoes with all the trimmings every week. He really didn't care that my diet had gone to shit, and I was growing sideways to almost 120 pounds.

My mom cared. She cursed my daddy out so badly when she bought new school clothes and none of them fit.

She said, "What the hell are you feeding my child over there? Got him looking like a little butterball!"

This was a red flag for my mother. She started making frequent random wellness checks to the house to make sure I was eating some vegetables.

She'd just pop up unexpectedly, which made my daddy furious, but she didn't care. She was coming to see about her baby, and she would ask me a bunch of questions about our living conditions.

It was like she was waiting for me to signal her, like: "If you're in danger, Son, blink twice." But I never did.

To this day, I still don't know why the hell I stayed. As if the canned rice, Fiesta shoes, and loaded baked potato coma weren't enough, wait till you hear what this nigga did next!

"One event, situation, circumstance, habit, addiction, crime, goal, or dream always triggers the next one."

CHAPTER 5

GOING OUT OF TOWN

When you get something new, it usually comes with a set of instructions; the unfortunate thing about parenting is there is no template, blueprint, or set of instructions for parenting. Most of the time, parents are just winging it and hoping for the best.

Parenting styles are different because kids are different. You can have three kids in the same family, and they'll all have their own unique, distinct personalities. I have nine kids. I have one child that I can just look at and they will fall in line, and others, I have to threaten their life with a weapon before they obey me.

Through trial and error, parents learn how to effectively engage and communicate with their children based on their personality types and learning styles. Though no one in the history of parenting has done it perfectly, some people should have just left well enough alone.

Yes, I'm talking about my daddy. He should have left me where the hell I was (or rather, I should have stayed where the hell I was) instead of taking a walk on the wild side.

I know you're thinking: "I haven't heard anything that bad about your daddy. He seems like a normal delusional bachelor trying to navigate his way through parenthood, just like everyone else."

My father was only thirty years old when I moved in with him, and his age played a huge factor in his ignorance. Thirty is such a delicate age. You're too young to be a master at anything and too damn old to still be making bad decisions.

Well, my father was a thirty-year-old phenomenon because he was a master at making bad decisions. Not all of his decisions were bad, but let's just say his judgment was a little off at times.

Let me explain…

I had been living with my dad for a couple of months now. We'd had some good days and some bad days, but none like the day he came into my room after midnight and dropped a bomb on me. I was fast asleep when his deep dark voice awakened me with a dumb-ass question.

"Are you asleep?"

I was like, "Of course I'm sleep. It's late and I have school in the morning!"

Long story short, he proceeded to tell me that he was about to go out of town without me! For some reason, he thought it was a good idea to leave his ten-year-old son in the house in the middle of the night without any adult supervision. Well, adults did show up randomly, but not the kind of adults you'd leave around your kids!

But I digress...

Our conversation went something like this:

Daddy: Look. I'm about to go out of town.

Me: But I've got school in the morning.

Daddy: Shit, I know you got to go to school. I said I'm going out of town. I ain't said nothing about you.

Me: So what am I about to do?

Daddy: You're going to stay here.

Me: By myself?

Daddy: Yeah. When you wake up, eat a bowl of Fruity O's and go to school.

Me: You're leaving me here, alone?

Daddy: What? You scared?

Me: Yes, I'm scared. I'm ten! I ain't never been alone in the house before! What's wrong with you?

(My daddy pulled out a black-and-white two-shot Derringer gun and put it on the table.)

Daddy: Here, if somebody comes into the house, you know what to do.

Me: No, I do not know what to do! Who have you been talking to that told you I know what to do? I'm a kid!

(My daddy completely ignored my obvious anxiety, fear, questions, and concerns. He proceeded to give me further instructions.)

Daddy: This is all preliminary. I got some other things I need you to do.

(He repositioned himself and moved in closer to make direct eye contact with me. I knew it was gonna be some bullshit because he started whispering at this point.)

Daddy: Now, some people are going to knock on this back door. Open the door for them, but keep the chain on the door. The price is $15. I want you to take their money, go upstairs, get one of the pills out of my box, give it to them, and lock the door after each sale. I'll see you tomorrow.

He left abruptly, and I was thinking, "Yeah, right! My daddy playing. There is no way he is asking me to sell pills to strangers in the middle of the night."

I shrugged it off and went back to sleep. At about 12:35 AM, I heard someone knocking at the back door, *DOO-DOO-DOO-DOO-DOO!*

I walked to the door, put some bass in my voice, and said, "What's up?" The buyer asked for pills. I did the transaction like my dad instructed me and went back to sleep.

A few moments later, I heard, *Doo-doo-doo-doo-doo!* The same thing happened. I did the business and went back to sleep.

Doo-doo-doo-doo-doo!

I said, "This goddamn door is cracking! I've got to go to school in the morning."

People were buying pills throughout the night. Needless to say, I didn't get any sleep. I went to school tired as hell the next day. After a series of naps and uncontrollable snoring, I was sent to the principal's office. When I got home, my dad was mad at me because he got a call from the school.

He said, "Why am I receiving phone calls about you sleeping in class?"

I said, "I don't know if you checked your little box upstairs, but it's full of money because your door was busy last night."

My daddy said, "Shit, it was like that?" Excitedly, he went upstairs to check his box.

Now, this was the moment I should have gotten on the rotary phone, called my mother, and said, "I'm going to meet you on the corner with my belongings." But I didn't because I was sleepy. I went to my room to take a nap.

Even if I had told my mother what was happening and moved back in with her, it would have been too late. The damage was done. The domino had fallen.

My father had already planted an unrighteous hustle in me. I experienced firsthand that I could make a lot of money in a short amount of time by selling drugs. It didn't matter that it was immoral or illegal or that I only did it that one time. It was engraved in my mind that selling drugs was profitable and there were no consequences. To my knowledge, my father was never arrested or harassed by the police.

The craziest thing about my father's side hustle was that it was totally unnecessary. My father was a successful entrepreneur with a booming business. He had a courier service that was doing very well.

He had more money than my mother. He owned multiple cars, wore tailored suits, and lived in an upscale apartment. He fed me baked potatoes, powdered milk, and Fruity O's because he was cheap, not because he was broke. He was even sending money back to his family in Louisiana.

Now, I don't know if the extra money he had was because of his courier service or his criminal activity. Nevertheless, selling drugs was a choice he made simply because of greed.

I really didn't know how broad my father's business was; all I knew was he sold these little white pills. Of course, with time, that changed into something more powerful and more profitable.

This is the heart and soul of the domino effect. One event, situation, circumstance, habit, addiction, crime, goal, or dream always triggers the next one.

Whether it leads to profit or poverty, progression or degression, building up or tearing down, it all works the same way. Once one domino falls, the others will follow, and it's almost impossible to stop the progression.

Now, this is the part of the story when I found out my daddy sold cocaine...

So, I was having tooth problems. My wisdom teeth were cutting through my gums, and I was in a lot of pain. I came downstairs because I heard my daddy in the kitchen. He was sitting at the table with his two friends, Ivory and James, who I knew pretty well because they were always around.

The whole scene looked like an assembly line. They had a Cool Whip container filled with white powder and these little plastic vials. They were filling the vials with white powder and stacking them neatly in a pile. There was money all over the table, and Ivory and James had on gun holsters, but nobody had a shirt on, including my daddy.

I was saying to myself, "Boy, this is a gangster-ass game of Monopoly they're playing."

I was too young and innocent to realize this was some high-level criminal activity going on here. I was also in too much pain to accurately assess the situation.

I walked into the kitchen to tell my dad about my toothache, hoping to get some Tylenol™, Robitussin™, or something to ease the pain. Instead, I got James's goofy ass trying to be a dentist.

He said, "Shit, let me see. Oh, I see the problem. His teeth are cutting in the back."

My daddy summoned me over to him, and told me to open my mouth. He took a close look, then dipped his finger into the white substance and placed it on my teeth.

Yes, you read that right. My daddy put pure uncut cocaine on my teeth! The pain was gone, but my whole face went numb. It took days before the feeling in my cheek came back.

I still can't believe I survived living with this crazy man. My father just wasn't ready to be a parent.

I stayed with my father from age ten to fourteen, which are undoubtedly the most influential years of a young man's life. This is the time when a boy begins his transition into manhood. It's also when boys begin to tower over their mothers and test their patience. Having a father or a father figure in the house during this time is critical.

Men are generally better at keeping teenage boys in check and helping them navigate puberty, raging hormones, rebellion, and temptation. I was stubborn, strong-willed, and flip at the mouth by nature.

My dad knew exactly how to check me without breaking me. My mother would have just punched me in the face, and I would have had to go see the dentist for real.

When I lived with my father, I was exposed to a lot of negatives, like promiscuous women, drugs, guns, Fruity O's, and illegal ways to make money.

On the contrary, I was also exposed to positives, like entrepreneurship, stewardship, manhood, fatherhood, and friendship. The way we live our lives before our children causes them to emulate us or reject us.

Over time, kids determine which parental traits they want to throw away and which traits they want to keep. With my dad, there was a lot to throw away, but I've learned to use the bad experiences to help make me a better parent.

Nevertheless, I know some of the seeds that were planted in me by my father were harmful. Those seeds produced a harvest in my life that should not have been. Just because a seed is planted doesn't necessarily mean it will grow. I was the one who brought the sunshine, the rain, and a whole lot of shit to make those seeds grow and blossom in my life. As much as I'd like to blame my father for my bullshit—I can't.

Instead, I'll just blame Willie!

“I have never met a good Willie, ever.”

CHAPTER 6

OFF TRACKSUIT

After living with my dad for over four years, I moved back in with my mother. My father didn't do anything to warrant my decision. There was no incident that made me say, "This was the last straw." We didn't get into an argument, nor were we on bad terms. I just missed my mother and sisters and was ready for a change. Though my father wasn't the best parent, he still was a good dude.

I learned a lot of valuable lessons from my father, some of which I use to govern my life today. For example, my dad said, "You ain't got to work for nobody." So I've never worked for anybody.

He said, "Always be clean and fresh." So I'm always clean and fresh.

The realist most gangsta shit my daddy ever said to me was, "Don't hope, hustle. The same shit you do for somebody else, you can do for your goddamn self." He told me to never hope that someone would put me on or do me a favor, but to work hard, hustle, and do it for myself. He taught me to be a man and make my own way because no one is gonna look out for me like I'm gonna look out for myself.

In life, you might get lucky enough to have some family and friends that are faithful to you and have your best interest at heart, but you can't always count on that.

At some point, you have to start making moves that benefit you, your family, and your future. There is nothing wrong with being intentional and even selfish when it comes to getting what you want in life. Now, I'm not saying you should go do something illegal or immoral to win in life. I've learned that this is not the way, and when you know better, you do better. But in the 1980s, that was exactly what I was saying! I got my bag by any means necessary because the clock was ticking and I was running out of time!

Let me explain...

My mama has this slogan she has been saying since I was ten years old: "You got to get your ass out my house at eighteen."

She'd been saying this for as long as I can remember. Anytime I did something bad and got into trouble, that was my mother's go-to phrase. She'd say, "You know something? Don't even fucking worry about it because you gone get your ass out of here at eighteen."

Parents must watch what they say to their children; please don't give your children this ultimatum. Not only is it the wrong thing to say, but it puts unnecessary pressure and stress on your kids that might cause them to run in the wrong direction. I know someone who forced their son out of the house at twenty, and he just wasn't ready.

He resorted to committing armed robbery to pay his rent and is currently doing a thirty-year prison sentence. The wrong advice coupled with the wrong mentality always equates to the wrong situation and outcome.

It's a domino effect that starts with ignorant parents. I'm not talking about ignorance like someone being rude or unruly. I'm simply talking about a lack of proper parental knowledge.

Children mature differently, and every child is not prepared, mature, or responsible enough to be on their own at age eighteen.

I believe this mindset started with the way our parents were raised. Most of them had to quit school and get a job in their early teens. They were already living on their own and possibly even married by the age of eighteen. Being out of the house by eighteen was the norm in the 1950s, '60s, and '70s. Over time, African Americans became more established, ambitious, and educated. Our kids were encouraged to finish high school and attend college. As a result, they were less prepared to be thrown into adulthood and fend for themselves. To tell a child they must be on their own by the age of eighteen can be terrifying. It was for me. Hence, it was the beginning of my street pharmaceutical life.

Have you ever been at the wrong place at the wrong time and met the wrong person, knowing full well if you just had not been there, your whole life would have taken a different route? Well, it happened to me. My mom moved into these very nice apartments, but the tenants were ignorant as hell. I became friends with this dude named Jeffrey, who was always on punishment.

One day, I was outside kicking it with Jeffrey, and this dude named Willie pulled up. Side note: I have never met a good Willie, ever. Anyway, Jeffrey and I were sitting in the park, and Willie pulled up in a Cutlass. It was his mama's Cutlass, but he was acting like it was his.

In the '80s, there were a lot of weird-looking dudes that gave a lot of badass advice. Willie was both weird looking and full of bad advice. He was a typical '80s cat: flashy, flakey, greasy, and loud.

No one in the '80s had good dental insurance, so Willie had an extra row of teeth on the bottom like a piranha. He also had a bushy Jheri curl.

Remember them people who had Jheri curls that didn't take all the way? They had the Jheri but no curl. That was Willie. His hair was nappy and wet with activator at the same time. To make matters worse, he wore a green visor with white trimming. He looked like a card dealer, but he was a drug dealer. I didn't know that yet, but I'm just saying.

Nevertheless, slick Willie had on something that did pique my interest. He had on a fresh-ass tracksuit.

In the '80s, everyone wore tracksuits, and Willie was wearing one of the best I'd ever seen. I was like, "His teeth fucked up, but that tracksuit is fresh as shit." Willie got out of the car and walked over to Jeffery.

He said, "What's up, Jeffrey baby? Who is this you got with you?"

Jeff replied, "This is my potna, Ali. He just moved around here. He used to stay with his daddy."

Then Willie looked right at me and said, "Who is you, nigga?"

Somewhat surprised, I said, "He just told you. I'm Ali and I just moved here. I was living with my daddy."

Willie replied, "You been living with your daddy? Oh, that's wild. This boy got a daddy. Ain't that some crazy shit?"

I thought to myself, "Don't everybody have a daddy? I was like, this nigga is ugly and dumb at the same time."

Willie asked me what I did for a living. I told him, "Nothing yet. I'm just fourteen."

He said, "Age ain't nothing to do with it. Everybody around here hustles."

I told him I didn't need to hustle because my momma had a good job.

He said, "No, nigga. You're going to want shit. You're going to definitely want some shit. I see you with your goddamn grocery store shoes on. You look like you got a job with them workman pants on." I forgot to mention that in addition to the shoes, my dad also bought my pants from the grocery store.

Willie went on to say, "You must cut grass or something with them ugly-ass Fiesta pants on." Then he continued to go in on me for about ten minutes straight, and everyone was laughing.

I ain't never been talked about before, and Willie kept talking shit. My neck was tight. I didn't like it. I didn't like none of that shit at all. I couldn't even say anything because he had that fresh-ass tracksuit on. I was like, "Damn."

The whole situation had me thinking. Willie said, "Everybody around there hustles." This resonated with me because my father always said, "Don't hope, hustle."

I asked Willie, "What do y'all do?"

He said, "Man, we sell dope."

In my innocence, I said, "You're supposed to say no to drugs. I've seen the commercials with the crime dog. He says to just say no."

Then Willie's crooked-teeth, dry-wet-hair ass said the most profound thing. He said, "Boy, we ain't using it, we selling it! And we ain't selling it to nobody who don't want it."

That shit made so much sense to me. Plus, I saw it with my own eyes the night my father left me home alone. His back door was popping with customers looking for drugs. Now my wheels were turning and I was thinking, "I got to get my ass out of my mama's house at eighteen. I only got four more years to get my shit together."

In my fourteen-year-old mind, the word *hustle* meant "to sell drugs." My daddy hustled, James and Ivy hustled, Willie hustled, and all the guys in my new neighborhood hustled. I guess I needed to hustle too. Sounded like a quick come-up. The pay was good, plus, I'd get to wear fresh-ass tracksuits. "Fuck it, I'm in!" I thought. I fell for it—hook, line, and sinker. That was the moment I decided to become a street pharmaceutical rep, hence making the biggest mistake of my life. I knocked down the domino that ultimately led to my demise. But it didn't start that way. It never does. It went a little something like this…

“There are no ifs, ands, buts, or maybes. Something will go down, and nine times out of ten, it’s you.”

CHAPTER 7

STREET PHARMACEUTICAL REP

The first day on the job as a drug dealer is quite different from the first day in the corporate world. There's no job interview, résumé, or first-day orientation. No one welcomes you to the team, hands you a new employee manual, and takes you out to lunch. You are just thrown to the wolves and have to learn to fend for yourself.

It's on-the-job training, and the learning curve is a muthafucker. If you fail, the consequences are jail or death. Now, death is optional, but jail is inevitable. You can go to jail early, or you can go to jail late—either way, you are going to jail.

With that being said, why on earth would anybody want to hustle for a living? Well, probably because the job is simple and the pay is exceptional. Notice I said the job is simple, not easy. Actually, this shit is a lot harder than people think.

All that shit you see on TV when somebody starts selling dope and then all of a sudden they're Nino Brown or a kingpin is false. It just doesn't work that way.

This is not the movies. Wesley Snipes is not running the cartel; he's running from the IRS. If you didn't know, Denzel went home after filming *Training Day*. Please don't get it twisted.

The reason why I tell my stories the way I tell them is because people tend to glorify the streets. Ain't nothing glorious about it. The streets can kill you, ruin your life, or both. The sad part is it doesn't just affect you. It affects the whole community, the culture, as well as the overall advancement of Black people.

It's a serious matter, and I'm never going to make light of it. I'm going to tell you the hard shit, the real shit, and the true shit. You can do what you want with the information. I just want these young boys to know: You can get into this shit if you want to. Just know some shit is going to happen to you. There are no ifs, ands, buts, or maybes. Something *will* go down, and nine times out of ten, it's you.

Now that I've gotten the disclaimer out of the way, let's get to the heart of the matter.

As N.W.A. would say, "You are now about to witness the strength of street knowledge," for which I had absolutely none.

When you start selling drugs, you are given a fifty pack. Everybody starts with a fifty. Out of the fifty, you can make anywhere from $110 to $120, depending on how you cut it. The thing is, you don't know that because ain't nobody walking you through an introduction to dope sales. My only reference was my friend Jeffrey, but he was little to no help because he was always on punishment. He told me how to get started.

I got my first fifty from this dude named Rannell. He supplies all the young boys in the neighborhood. He is like the G-Money of his crew, but there's a dude that's above him. That's the big man that you don't want to run into.

I was young, naïve, and extremely wet behind the ears, but I was ready to start my pharmaceutical sales initiation process. Rannell was in the center of the block, sitting on a red scooter with a Tek-9 strapped across his chest.

I walked over to him with my goofy ass like, "Hey, you Rannell?"

He said, "Nigga, who is you?"

I said, "I'm Ali. I just moved over here. I was living with my daddy. They said I'm supposed to get a fifty from you."

Rannell said, "Nigga, do you even sell dope?"

I said, "No, not until you give it to me."

Rannell gave me a fifty pack and warned me, "You better bring my money back, little nigga. This situation is motherfucking life or death."

I said, "You sound just like my momma."

Rannell said, "What?" and put his hand on his gun. That was my cue to get the hell out of his face.

I had the fifty but had no clue what was next. I didn't know if you were supposed to sell it for $60, give Rannell $50, and I keep $10 or what. Jeffrey told me I had to cut the fifty up with a razor. He showed me how he cut it and instructed me to cut it up in nickels, dimes, and twenties.

Once again, open mouth, insert foot: I said, "Man, I took a ceramics class, and this doesn't look like enough dope to make nickels and dimes."

He said, "Boy, you ain't making no damn ceramic pieces. I'm going to show you." So Jeffrey cut up my dope and put it on the table. Now, I had to find a way to package it. Jeffrey used a matchbox, but I used a film container to put all my dope in.

I was ready to make my first sale. I ain't going to lie. I was nervous as hell. Not to mention I had no clue what I was doing. Jeffrey was like, "Come on, man! Let's get out there!"

It was nothing like the setup in *New Jack City*. It wasn't organized where people came to a window to get their drugs. I was out there on a street corner in plain sight where the police could see me, or even worse, my mother!

So I was posted up, and there was lots of traffic. People were just out there like ants running into each other, and it was a lot of busyness going on. Everybody was walking up, getting their shit, and then walking off. People were coming up with money in their hands. The transactions were happening so fast and frequently I didn't know when to get in.

It was like everybody had their customers. I was like, "Oh, that's you right there? Okay, cool. Oh, she came to you like three times already; that's you."

Jeffery said, "Hey, you're going to have to get out there, man." I decided to just jump in. This dude walked up to me and was like, "Hey, what's up?"

I said, "What's up with you?" Now, he was looking at me and I was looking at him.

I turned and said to Jeffrey, "Is he supposed to say something? Or am I supposed to say something to him?"

Jeffery told me to get the fuck out the way because I was tripping.

Jeffrey made the sale and disappeared. He left me on the corner with Willie, but I was still struggling to make a sale—not because the customers weren't coming, but because I had no clue what I was doing. I learned rather quickly that drug addicts are very impatient and quite rude!

At this point, I was frustrating the dealers and the addicts. Willie told me, "Hey, man, this side ain't for you. Go down the street where the cars are with your silly ass."

I went down by the cars, and people were pulling up, and dealers were selling drugs to the people in cars. This looked a lot easier to me.

I walked up to a car that pulled up. I put two rocks in my hand because I wanted to give people choices. I valued the importance of customer service. So, I said, "What's happening, man? What do you need?"

I put my hand in the car, and the man hit my hand. The rocks flew up in the air, fell into his car, and drove off. Jeffrey said, "Hey, man, did you just put your hand in that car?"

I said, "Yeah."

"Did you have some dope in your hand?"

I said, "Yeah."

"That man popped your hand, didn't he?"

I said, "Yeah. But I think he's going to come around and come back."

Jeffrey said, "Man, that man ain't coming back. Have you paid Rannell yet?"

I said, "Paid him what?" Again, my response was as dumb as the box of rocks I was selling or attempting to sell.

At the time, I had no idea how great of an offense this was and that my life was on the line. This is how many young drug dealers get killed within weeks or even days of being on the job. Their lives are destroyed because they don't understand the game. They get jacked, or they are just not cut out for it and end up owing the big man money.

By the grace of God, I survived because Jeffrey helped me out. He said, "Man, come over here. Put all your dope down right here. Now, this is a matter of life and death. You can't lose any more dope." I could tell by the look on his face that he wasn't joking.

As stated before, this shit is not easy. People tend to think that it's easy, which is the irony of the whole business. The people watching you get cash, cars, clothes, women, and fresh-ass tracksuits think it's easy money and want in—not to mention all the rappers that have glorified, endorsed it, and made it a trend.

But it's not easy because there are no clean sales. There are no honest dealers, addicts, or kingpins. All of that shit is criminal activity. The person who's smoking it is a criminal, and so are you. So it's not going to be a fair business. This false advertisement was the downfall of many Black men in the '80s and '90s. Countless men lost their families, their freedom, and their very lives in this shit.

This domino effect was the most damaging and devastating thing to ever hit the Black community.

Slavery was horrible because we were put in chains, but the crack epidemic was different because somehow, we were convinced to put the chains on ourselves. It was the sneakiest form of systemic racism to date.

Closing the plants that gainfully employed uneducated Black men in the '70s, introducing the welfare system that encouraged Black women to dump their husbands, and then infesting our neighborhoods with cheap drugs in the '80s was genius and evil at the same time.

They knew that all these out-of-work, depressed, lonely men were going to either become addicted to drugs or sell drugs to win back their families. Either way, it was total annihilation and sudden death for an already oppressed people.

I'm sad to say that I participated in this debacle. At least I escaped with my life, but there was still a price to pay. There's always a price to pay. You may not see the upfront cost, but eventually, you will have to pay up!

> *"I had to somehow find the silver lining in this situation."*

CHAPTER 8

YOUNGSTER

Since my first night on the block was a disaster, Jeffrey gave me a dope-selling-for-dummies crash course. This boosted my confidence, but not as much as seeing Willie bust out with another fresh-ass tracksuit. I was like, if Willie can succeed at doing this shit, I know I can. There was absolutely nothing to fear but fear itself. I had the knowledge, the product, and even an alias.

The older dope boys gave me the nickname "Youngster" because I was the youngest dealer on the block. So after watching *Scarface* a few times and listening to N.W.A.'s "Dope Man" on repeat on my Walkman, I was ready to make my first sale.

Making your first dope sale is equivalent to having sex for the first time. You're anxious and excited to do it because you know it's gonna feel good. In your mind, it's just a physical act, but it's more than that. Sex is physical, spiritual, emotional, mental, and transactional, and once you cross the line, there's no turning back.

Selling dope works the same way. It's not just a physical act. It's spiritual because drugs take people to another realm mentally. It's emotional because criminal activity is stressful and makes you paranoid. It's emotional because you're selling to people in your community, and you know you're negatively impacting people you may know. I can go on, but you get the picture.

Like sex, you'll always remember your first time.

In the dope game, you always remember your first sale. You will never forget the person that solidified your title as a dope man, weed man, coke man, or whatever narcotics you're selling. Let me share with you how I broke my dope-selling virginity. It was actually a threesome, but I didn't know that going in.

KIRK & GWEN

I was standing on the corner, and this dude named Kirk walked up to me and said, "What's up, Youngster? You got some?"

Like a dummy, I said, "Some what?"

He said, "Man, let me get a dime from you."

Now, this seemed like a simple transaction and a clean sale, until it wasn't. I walked closer to him, and then I turned my back because I didn't want nobody hitting my shit like last time. I gave him the dime. He gave me $10. I was like, "Cool, we're good." I turned around, and this lady was standing in my path.

I said, "Hey, how you doing?"

And, bam! She punched me in the goddamn jaw.

I punched her back. I was like, "Bitch! What you doing?" Then Kirk jumped on my back and wrestled me to the ground. I couldn't believe I was getting jumped by a goddamn dope fiend couple.

I told them, "I'm fourteen. What the hell is wrong with y'all?" I got away from them and started walking fast.

I was coming through the neighborhood pissed! I was like, "What the fuck?"

I saw Jeffrey. He saw that my face was flustered and said, "Man, what's wrong with you?"

I said, "I sold a dime to this dude, and then this lady hit me in the jaw."

He said, "Oh, Kirk and Gwendolyn? Ain't no clean sales with them. You see Kirk, you got to watch for Gwen. You see Gwen, you got to watch Kirk. They wild!"

I said, "Why didn't you tell me there's a dope fiend couple out here jumping on people?"

I should have just quit right then, but I couldn't let Kirk and Gwen break my spirit. I had to somehow find the silver lining in this situation. I didn't get jacked; I made my first sale, and I kicked both of their crackhead asses. So in actuality, I got the title, and I won. I felt like a champ until I met the real champ.

CHAMP

Same day, different crackhead. I was walking through the neighborhood and ran into an addict named Champ. Now Champ was not the typical skinny, weak, frail-looking crackhead. Champ was a big dude. He was around five-six and three hundred pounds and was a known dope biter. A *dope biter* is someone who asks to examine your rocks, bites your dope, then holds it in their mouth so they can smoke it later.

The hustlers on the block know Champ and what he does, so they don't fuck with him. My dumb ass was trying to buy a tracksuit, so I served him. Champ walked up and said, "Hey, Youngster, let me get something, man. Shit!"

I said, "What do you need?"

He said, "Man, let me see what you got, baby."

Now, my first mind said, "Don't do it." But as you know, I have a history of making bad decisions. I reluctantly handed Champ a rock. He examined it, and like the dope-biting crackhead he was, he bit it.

Then he said to me, "Nah, that's too small, player."

I said, "No, muthafucker. It was bigger before you bit it. Champ, I ain't taking that shit! You bit that shit. It's yours!"

He said, "I ain't paying for that; it's too small."

I said, "Champ, don't play with my intelligence."

He said, "You better get the fuck out of my face."

I saw that this conversation was going nowhere, so I swung on Champ. Champ dodged my punch like a professional boxer. He grabbed me by the collar, picked me up, and this muthafucker threw me into a dumpster. I wasn't even by a dumpster. The man threw me in a dumpster like he was shooting free throws.

One minute I was fighting a dope fiend couple, and the next minute I was lying in a goddamn dumpster. How's that for the first day on the job?

In the '80s, people drank malt liquor in forty-ounce bottles called *forties.* As soon as I landed in the dumpster, I felt an empty forty underneath me. I picked up the forty, threw it at Champ, and burst him in the back of his head.

POW!

Champ said, "Goddam, Youngster! All this behind some crack?"

I said, "No, muthafucker, it's because you threw me in a goddamn dumpster."

My friend Denard saw me coming through the hood, walking fast and talking to myself. I was trying to make sense of all of this.

He said, "Hey, boy, I saw you get thrown in that dumpster. Was it Champ?"

I said, "Yeah, how do you know?"

He said, "That muthafucker threw me in a dumpster last week. This shit hot out here, ain't it, boy?"

I told Denard, "I don't think I'm cut out for this shit. I'm emotional, paranoid, defensive, and angry. I'm going through a lot of shit."

I see why drug dealers are so quick to bust a cap in a muthafucker. They're under a lot of stress and pressure. They don't have time for additional bullshit. Though my first day on the job should have been my last day on the job, I'm not a quitter, so I hung in there. The next few days were somewhat civilized, profitable, and quite comical. Crackheads are, without question, some of the funniest people on the planet. My biggest laugh came from Byron…the battery snatcher.

THE BATTERY SNATCHER

I was fourteen years old. I didn't have a driver's license, a car, or a bicycle. This didn't stop Byron from walking up to me with a car battery. I immediately told him to step off when I saw him coming with this bullshit.

He said, "Now, Youngster, look, don't start with this shit now. This is a brand-new-ass battery."

I said, "I don't have a car, man. What am I going to do with a car battery?"

He began to make his case. He said, "You don't have a car now, but eventually, you're gonna get a car. You're out here making money, but if you want to impress the girls, you're gonna need a car, and you're going to need this battery."

This nigga missed his calling. He should have been a lawyer because he almost convinced me to buy this battery. I was standing there contemplating, but it was short-lived.

This man I'd never seen before started yelling, "Byron! Byron!" Suddenly, Byron took off, running at full speed with the car battery. The dude was like, "Byron, you better bring my motherfucking battery back, bitch!"

Byron had tried to sell me a stolen car battery!

The dude started chasing Byron, and I became an eyewitness to a high-speed foot chase. Ain't no way ole dude was catching Byron though. Byron was running like Usain Bolt, and the nigga never dropped the battery. The shit is fucking ridiculous what I went through and what I saw on a daily basis. Have you ever seen a domino presentation where the dominos are rapidly falling simultaneously in multiple directions? This is what it's like being on the block. Everything is happening so fast. Some of it makes you laugh, some of it makes you cry, and all of it is ridiculous, ignorant bullshit. People are destroyed for a lack of knowledge.

We were ignorant and totally oblivious about the impact crack would make on the African American community. I even believe the perpetrators underestimated how effective the crack epidemic would be. It was like dropping a nuclear bomb on an entire race of people and watching it implode.

One moment we were enjoying growing up in the '80s and playing till the streetlights came on, and then the next moment we were dodging drive-by shootings and getting robbed by random crackheads. Everything and everyone were affected—the rich, the poor, music, fashion, films, politics, education, entrepreneurs, homeowners, families, dealers, addicts, how we saw ourselves, and ultimately how others saw African Americans as a whole. It was all fucked up.

As a dealer, I was blindsided by the money and the dream of being financially independent. No one told me how it would all go down. No one told me about the smoking gun.

SMOKING GUN

I was on the corner doing my thing, and this dude came through and said, "Hey, Youngster, I see what you got popping. Come on by my place. I got this white girl smoking like a motherfucking chimney. Pull up and you can get your shit off."

Being the paper chaser that I was, I went over to his place. He wasn't lying. A white girl was there smoking like a chimney, and she had friends, lots of them. So I was over there serving them rock after rock. They were buying and smoking, smoking and buying. The shit was crazy.

This dude was smoking his shit, and this nigga exhaled and blew a large amount of crack smoke in my face. That shit ran me hot! I've seen dealers turn into addicts, and it's never a pretty picture. It's almost always dangerous and destructive. N.W.A. said it best in "Dopeman":

To be a dope man, boy, you must qualify.
Don't get high off your own supply.

This quote originated from the movie *Scarface*. It was code for me and a HUGE trigger. I was extremely offended by what he had done.

I was like, "Are you trying to get me high, nigga?" He didn't answer, so I just hit him. I punched him square in the face.

We started fighting, and his gun fell out of his jacket. It was a .25 automatic. I had never held a gun besides my daddy's little Deringer. I picked the gun up, and I wasn't even holding the gun correctly, but that didn't matter. I was just gonna live in the moment.

I start saying shit I've only heard on TV. I said, "Freeze! Everybody down! Don't make me pop y'all asses."

I guess I sounded convincing because everybody got down on the ground. I was like, "I got the power! They're listening." So I talked some more shit and walked slowly out the door. Then I took off running like a bat out of hell.

Now, I had my first gun, which was not good. When you are out there doing wrong and you get a gun, it gives you a false sense of security and confidence. The problem is, you're not the only one with a gun. The dealers have guns; the addicts have guns; the police have guns, and when you're constantly being tested, pressured, and disrespected, eventually, you're gonna use that gun.

In an instant, you can go from a drug dealer trying to make a quick buck to a murderer with someone's blood on your hands. Worst-case scenario, you can be murdered and sent to an early grave. Karma is real. Once you start shooting at people, you're gonna get shot at. It's inevitable and only a matter of time.

Remember, I said once the dominoes start falling, it's hard to stop the progression. In the dope game, things always become progressively worse. Most of the time, we don't see it coming because we get blinded by the cash, clothes, cars, and guns we carry. Progress often comes with prosperity. Mine started with a rainbow and ended with a pot of gold.

TINK

I was in the park with Rannell, getting fronted another fifty pack. This gay dude named Tink walked up, or should I say pranced up, because he was a sissy. This was the '80s. You could call gays "sissy" back then. I know you can't do that now, but then, it was permitted.

Tink was the only gay dude that we knew in the neighborhood. We called him "Tink the Sissy." Now, Tink was more funny than gay. Tink was so goddamn funny to me. He came to the park wearing soft aerobic Reeboks, leg warmers, Carl Lewis shorts, a wet Jheri curl with a Coca-Cola cap, and a half shirt that read "Thriller."

Tink came up to Rannell and said, "Rannell, why do I have to keep walking over here to get my cracks? I don't like it. Why can't nobody sell crack over there in the apartment that I live in? I'm walking back and forth, back and forth. My little Reeboks is tore up."

Tink kept complaining that there were no dealers in his apartment complex, and he was tired of walking to the park to get his cracks. Tink went on to say, "You need to send some of your little crack workers over to the Greens." Tink made his purchase and pranced away.

Rannell ignored his request, but I heard him loud and clear. I'm smart, and I had already walked off. I knew how Tink walked to his apartment. I met Tink in the parking lot and said, "Tink."

He said, "What?"

I said, "Shit is popping over there like that?"

Tink replied, "Yes, we are over there. Do you want me to show you? I will show you."

So I walked over to the Greens apartments with Tink. He told me to stand by the pool and he would bring the customers to me. Ten minutes later, I knew why Tink's shirt read "Thriller," because them muthafuckers came out like zombies. Tink kept his word and brought them to me in droves. I was over there rolling. I was making so much money, and nobody knew how I was doing it. I thought I was the invisible man, but someone was watching. In the dope business, somebody is always watching.

THE BIG MAN

I was doing so well that I didn't get fronted a fifty from Rannell anymore. I just walked up and bought my dope directly. I was up to an ounce now. I went to the park to meet Rannell to buy an ounce, but on this day, Charles, a.k.a. Nino Brown, was there. Charles was the "big man." He was at the park, and he was trying to talk to me, and I didn't want to be talked to. I directed my attention toward Rannell to avoid eye contact with Charles. Charles said, "What's up, Youngster? I heard about you, man."

Ignoring Charles, I said, "Rannell, let me get that ounce."

Rannell said, "Charles is talking to you."

I said, "I hear him. I don't want to talk to him. Let me get that ounce so I can bounce."

Charles went on to say, "Hey, Youngster. You in my neighborhood selling a lot of drugs, man. What do you think about working with me?"

I told Charles that I didn't want to work for anybody. This man said, "Nah, Youngster. I don't think you really get what I'm saying. Everybody around here works for me. Either you work for me and I get my percentage, or you don't get any more product." Charles proceeded to pull out a Desert Eagle, which was the biggest gun I'd seen in my life. Then Charles said, "Youngster, what I'm saying is, you're going to work for me."

What Charles didn't realize was I'd been out there selling dope for four weeks now. I was way harder than he thought. I'd been galvanized by the streets. While Charles was talking shit with a gun on me, he didn't even see that I had reached into my pocket and pulled out my .25. I hit his ass with it. “No, I ain’t going to be selling for nobody, my man.”

Charles was tickled. He said, “Oh, this little nigga pulled a pistol on me. Boy, Rannell, you didn’t tell me this little nigga had a heart. Let me see your little pistol, nigga.” Charles effortlessly took my gun and said, “Nigga, you remind me of me when I was younger.”

Charles continued to chuckle, making a scene and drawing attention to the situation. Some of the other dealers started to gather around.

Excitedly, he told them, “This little mutherfucker just pulled a gun on me.”

Charles acted as if I had pulled out a water pistol, but my .25 had real bullets and could have done damage. Charles was so unbothered. He seemed more amused than anything. He even gave me my gun back. He was like, “Here you go, lil’ nigga.”

It was a friendly exchange that could have been deadly. It was by the grace of God that it didn’t go sideways. It ended with Charles saying, “Look, lil’ nigga, let me tell you something. If anybody fucks with you, let me know. If you ever need me, don't hesitate to call." He proceeded to tell all the dealers standing around not to fuck with me and just let me do my thing.

I appreciated the love that Charles had shown me, but I was a real one. I was a man's man, my own man. My daddy taught me how to be a man. How to protect and provide for myself and never work for anybody. What my father didn't teach me, the streets surely did. The streets is the best and worst teacher. Selling death had prepared me for life. With rocks in my hand, a gun on my waist, and a pocket full of money, I had an arrogant false peace. Though I appreciated the gesture, I really didn't need Charles. I just kept doing me because I thought I would never need him, until I did.

"Say, my man,
what's your name?"

CHAPTER 9

HOLDING GRUDGES

It was 1990, and I was fifteen years old. I was into girls, rap music, video games, and cheeseburgers, but I was also a drug dealer. I'd been in the game for over a year. Through trial and error, I'd figured some things out on my own.

Though the shit had not been easy, I'd had more good days than bad. I'd made a considerable amount of money, I'd never been jacked, and I'd successfully managed to keep my mom in the dark about what I was really doing after dark.

If my mother found out I was selling drugs, my ass was toast. I'm not sure what was worse: if she found out I was selling drugs or if she found out I was storing drugs in her house. Either way, it was in my best interest to make sure she never found out.

I know when she reads this book, I still might get a whooping.

She's older now, so I think I could take her, but back when I was a teenager, she could level my ass. At that point in time, I still hadn't grown much. I was patiently waiting for that adolescent growth spurt to happen for me. I expected that I would grow to at least six feet, like my dad and my uncles. Let's just say I'm still waiting on that shit to happen.

Nevertheless, at fifteen I was five seven and weighed about 150 pounds. I was small, but I still had the respect of everyone on the block. I was Youngster, and no one fucked with me. Charles commanded it, my swagger demanded it, and I wasn't scared of nobody except my momma.

Though I had hands and many fights, I never started a fight in my life. My motto was, "Don't start nothing, won't be nothing." For the most part, I never ran into many problems in my neighborhood because everyone knew me, but that was all about to change.

On this particular day, I got into an altercation with a dude named Quincy. Now, Quincy was the neighborhood, Debo—big, strong, cracked out, and utterly disrespectful. He was a certified bully that most dealers were afraid of, and for good reason. Quincy was the type of nigga that would beat you up, take your money and your crack, and smoke it in your face.

I was walking through the apartments, and Quincy saw me and said, “Hey, youngster. I know you’re holding. What’s up?”

Quincy was about six four, 260 pounds, and all muscle. I’d heard horror stories about this dude and had managed to avoid him for many months. Nevertheless, there I was standing face-to-face with this big Neanderthal-ass nigga.

I was like, “Fuck it!” so I said, “What’s up, Quincy? What do you need?” He said he wanted a dime.

I told him to throw his money on the ground first. He was offended and said, "Man, why are you trying to do me like that?"

I responded, "If you want a dime, just throw your money on the ground, and I'll set your dope on the sidewalk."

Quincy said, "Man, you're acting like I'm a motherfucking pigeon or something."

I said, "No, I'm acting like you are a jacker."

Quincy angrily balled his money up and threw it at me and said, "Here's your fucking money, nigga." I set his dime on the ground and walked away.

Quincy started yelling, "You're a whore-ass little boy for that." Now, Quincy was a grown-ass man calling me a whore-ass little boy.

Have you ever heard the phrase "defining moment"? Well, my encounter, or should I say my encounters with Quincy were defining moments for me. They identified something that I didn't know about myself. Quincy taught me that I, Ali Siddiq, am a grudge holder—not in a little way, but in a very big way. I'm not the type of grudge holder that will get you back just one time and be satisfied. No, muthafucker, I'm a when-I-see-you, every-time-I-see-you-its-onsite type of grudge holder.

The lapse in time does not matter to me. It might take a day, a week, or ten years for me to get you back, but I will get you back. Call me petty, call me vindictive, but when I catch your ass, call 911 because you're gonna need medical attention.

My first encounter with Quincy wasn't that bad. So what warranted the type of aggression that happened in our next encounter? Pagers are not like cell phones are today. Everybody didn't have them. The only people who had pagers were doctors and drug dealers. So I got paged, and it meant for me to go to the park to meet a customer.

The first pagers didn't have phone numbers. When you got paged, you knew to report to a specific location. I got to the park, and there was a dude named Pat at the park.

Pat said, "Yo, let me get something from you."

At this moment, I only had two rocks left. I also had $4,000 in my sock. This was going to be my last sale of the night. I told Pat, "I have two rocks."

He said, "Let me have them."

Unbeknownst to me, Pat and Quincy were brothers. As I was serving Pat, I got tapped on the shoulder. I turned around, and, bam! Quincy hit me with everything he had.

In movies, when you see people lifted up in the air after being hit, you think it's just a stunt and that shit can't happen in real life. Well, I'm here to tell you—yes, the fuck it can.

I got hoisted up in the air, and my body bounced up off the cement. While I was unconscious, Quincy took my last two rocks and all my money.

I couldn't see anything, but I could hear everything. I knew it was Quincy because when I landed, my ear was on the ground and I heard, "Click! Click! Click! Click! Click!"

I remembered when I saw Quincy earlier that day. He had dress shoes on. "Click! Click! Click!

Click! Click!" was all I heard as that nigga ran off with my shit.

Now, I was lying on the ground. My entire eyeball was flipped inside out and upside down. When I tried to open my eyes, all I saw was white. Today, I have a huge scar over my eye because Quincy broke five bones in my face and did permanent damage to my optic nerve.

As I lay there temporarily blind and in extreme pain, I had to somehow find a way to get help. I'd been in my neighborhood a long time, so I could walk through it with my eyes closed. I took a few moments to gather myself, and then I got up.

I proceeded to make my way through the neighborhood. My goal was to make it to the spot where Charles and his crew hung out. I knew if I could just make it to them, I would be okay. I was touching walls, cars, and mailboxes. I passed by the pool without falling in, and finally I made it to the spot where everyone was. When I got there, I collapsed to the ground.

Charles ran up and said, "Little nigga, what's wrong with you?"

I said, "Quincy, Quincy hit me in the eye."

He said, "I knew that muthafucker had just done something. I saw him running down the street a few minutes ago. Did that bitch have on dress shoes?"

I was rushed to the hospital and got patched up. As I was lying there, seeds of rage and revenge were festering in me.

Quincy was on my list, and by any means necessary, I was gonna get that bitch back.

That happened when I was fifteen. Fast-forward three years, and I was eighteen years old. There was a rapper in Houston by the name of Bun B. He had a crew in the '90s called the Middle Fingers. In the Middle Fingers, there's a dude named Danny. I tell true stories, so if you want to verify what I'm saying, you can.

Danny and I were in his mama's car. It was a Burgundy Beretta. We were driving down the street, and out of the corner of my eye, the good one, I saw a dude standing at the bus stop that looked like Quincy.

I said, "Yo, Danny, pull over right here and let me out."

He said, "Man, you don't stay around here."

I said, "I know where I stay. Let me out of the car."

He said, "What's up?"

I said, "Remember I told you about the man named Quincy who robbed and hit me in the face when I was fifteen. I just saw him at the bus stop. Let me out of the car."

He said, "Man, let that shit go."

I said, "I can't do that. Let me out and go home." Danny let me out of the car, and I walked toward the bus stop.

At the time, my gun of choice was a .38. I walked up to Quincy just to confirm it was him. I said, "My man, what's your name?"

He said, "Nigga, Quincy." Without hesitation, I shot him three times, spat in his face, and walked off.

To my surprise, Danny hadn't left. I walked back to the car and got in.

Danny looked at me and said, "Man, that's fucked up what you just did. You shot that man in my mama's car."

I said, "I didn't shoot that man in your mama's car. I shot that man outside of your mama's car, and I told you to go about your damn business."

That happened when I was eighteen.

At nineteen, I went to prison but for drug possession. My life of crime finally caught up with me. You can only get away with that shit for so long. It took five years for the inevitable to happen in my life, but it happened. Honestly, I deserved it and I'm grateful for it.

The life of a drug dealer ends in two ways: prison or death. Some are lucky enough to get in and get out unscathed, but the majority have to face a very certain fate.

I am blessed to have escaped with my life, but I lost my freedom in the process.

At twenty-two years old, I was in the Texas Department of Corrections, Darrington Unit. In prison, they have a brush called a *shitter brush*. This is what you clean the toilet with; that's why it's called the shitter. It's usually made of hard plastic or wood. I walked into the room and saw a familiar face sitting at the table.

I said, "Is that Quincy? That muthafucker lived?"

I picked up the shitter brush and said, "Say, my man, what's your name?"

He said, "Quincy, nigga." I hit him on top of his head and split his shit open. We started fighting, and I got him on the ground and kept punching him in the face. The officers came to break up the fight. It took multiple officers to get me off of him, and I was talking crazy.

"No, bitch, one of us got to go! I'm going to murder you and your mama!" I continued to go off.

I was moved to a different unit because of the altercation with Quincy.

They say that revenge is best served cold, and I was a cold muthafucker when it came to Quincy. I shot him, I busted his head, and I beat him profusely. You would think I'd be satisfied.

Well, I wasn't.

Last year, I was in Walmart with my mother, and I saw an old man with a walker.

I turned to my mom and said, "I need you to go to the car."

She said, "For what?"

I said, "Mama, go to the car."

"What's wrong?" she replied.

I said, "Remember that dude who hit me in my eye at fifteen? I just saw him. Now, go to the car."

I walked up to the old man and said, "Hey, my man. What's your name?"

He turned around and said, "Nigga, don't you hit me! I was on crack, and I am sorry."

You know something that I realized as I thought about all of this? I went to prison for six years. I got jumped on by a dope-fiend couple. I got thrown in a dumpster, got my eye messed up, and have been holding a grudge against a man all these years. And I realized I did all of that for a fresh-ass tracksuit.

> *"The cool thing about hustling is that it pleases the Almighty because you are operating in faith."*

CHAPTER 10

DON'T HOPE, HUSTLE

The only similarity between the words *hope* and *hustle* is that they both start with the letter *H*. Besides the letter, they have nothing in common and mean the exact opposite.

Hope has to do with feelings, emotions, expectations, dreams, and desires. Hope is a beautiful thing that has been romanticized since the beginning of time. It's seeing light at the end of the tunnel or imagining an outcome before it happens. When facing a challenge, hope brings peace and a positive attitude.

The problem with hope is that it has no substance. To hope means nothing more than to wish. When we make a wish, we are typically standing still, our eyes are closed, and we simply think positive thoughts. This is cute, but it's not going to change shit in your life. I believe this is why my father always said: "Don't hope, hustle."

The word hustle has gotten a bad rap over the years, but the truth is, everybody is a hustler in their profession. It doesn't matter if you're pushing education, electronics, blogs, books, crack, weed, or Mary Kay. If you're offering a product or service to consumers, you're a hustler. The product or service you offer may deserve the negative connotation, but not the hustle.

Hustling is not a feeling; it's a force. Hustle is not an attitude; it's a principle. To hustle means you are doing everything in your power to make something happen. Working, moving, learning, growing, investing, building, running, seeking, grinding, etc. When you are involved in these things, you are hustling.

Hustle moves obstacles and opposition out of the way. It's using your position, power, and persuasion to tip the scale in the direction you want it to go. Hustle means war. You are at war with yourself and all other opposing forces.

Most people prefer peace over war and hope over hustle. This is why the average person never reaches their full potential, because they don't want to do the work or go to war for it. The only way countries get bigger and stronger is through war, and the only way we make progress is through hustle.

Hope is a noun. Hustle is a verb. Hope is passive. Hustle is aggressive. Hope is grace. Hustle is faith. Hope is peace. Hustle is war. Hope stands still. Hustle forges ahead. Though they are different, both are good to fulfill your purpose, but only one is a necessity.

Oprah didn't hope she'd become a billionaire, nor did Stephen Curry hope he'd become the greatest shooter of all time. They hustled to make it happen. The bad thing about hustling is that it involves scrapes, bruises, and lots of failures. Elon Musk had multiple failed business ventures, but now he's the richest man in the world.

When you're running hard after something, you're going to fall, you're going to break something, and you're going to want to quit. This is why hope is the perfect partner to hustle. Hope changes your attitude about failure and causes you to want to move forward. Hustle and hope work together to propel you toward your destiny, but the greatest of the two is...hustle.

MOM

"Don't hope, hustle," has been my life's motto. It was first spoken to me by my father at ten years old. The first person I saw demonstrate this principle was my mother. It's a principle because it's the way she governed and fashioned her life. My mother got pregnant at seventeen years old, and for the most part had to hustle her way through life to achieve her goals.

When I was young, my mother was always working and going to school. Her work ethic enabled her to accomplish small goals as well as large goals, and it was easy to see the progression.

We went from living in a one-bedroom apartment to a two-bedroom. Then we moved to a townhouse and eventually into our own home.

My mother was never satisfied. She was always looking forward and reaching ahead. Though she never verbally told me to be a hustler, she inadvertently taught me to be one.

All the cards were stacked against her because she was young, poor, Black, female, single, and a mother. This made her a lot tougher than most women. Most people think I get my ruggedness from my father, but it came from my mother.

My mother played no games. She was structured, intentional, and always on her game. She knew exactly what moves to make to get her to the next level in life. She didn't let anyone or anything stop or delay her progress.

Friends, family, and foolish men were all collateral damage when it came to her advancement. She even sent her children away so that she could build momentum—so you know she wasn't going to take no shit from men.

My father's immaturity was a stumbling block for my mother, which is the reason their marriage didn't last. My mother took life seriously. She is the type of person that will give you grace and mercy for a season, but once that season is up, it's up. My mother can love you with all her heart one day and then leave your ass in the dust the next day, especially if you mistake her kindness for weakness. I am the exact same way.

Both my mother and I have this trigger in our brains that goes off when someone blatantly disrespects us. I've seen niggas try my mother; then after they regained consciousness, they never tried her again.

When I violently attacked Quincy in Darrington Unit, it wasn't new behavior; it was learned. I watched my mother go off on muthafuckers when I was younger. She was determined to give her kids a better life, and she didn't mind fighting, working, educating herself, or hustling to make it happen.

DAD

Now, my dad was a different type of hustler. My daddy had finesse, swag, and charisma. The beauty of it was most people didn't know they were being hustled; they just fell right into his hands.

He also hustled for different reasons. My dad didn't hustle to dig his way out of a hole, but rather to keep himself from falling into one. He had an established way of living that he wanted to maintain. He liked nice cars, clothes, cash, cribs, and beautiful women, so he did what he had to do to continue to have access to the things he liked.

My dad also took care of his family in Louisiana. He wanted to have enough money to help them in their time of need.

My daddy had a thriving, legal business, as well as an illegal one. In addition to this, he worked odd jobs and was always looking for ways to make extra money.

My father was an entrepreneur and was 100 percent against working for "The Man." It didn't matter if the man was White, Black, yellow, or green. He wasn't going to do it. He fully understood the power of financial freedom, living life on your own terms, being your own boss, and not having an institution put a cap on your salary or your time.

During the four years I lived with my father, I watched him go to work every single day with no days off. He was always moving, snatching, grabbing, and going. Though he wasn't as structured as my mother, there was still a science in how he moved.

He understood that to get new business opportunities, he had to look like a professional. This is why he wore tailored suits with perfectly shined shoes and a nice watch. He made you want to do business with him because he was polished. His appearance, his swagger, and his conversation were all a part of his hustle. My daddy was like "the boogie man," he was out to get you.

My father taught me that men go out and get it. Men take care of their families.

This threw me for a loop because there were times in my life when my father was absent. Taking care of your family is so much more than sending a paycheck. It's being there physically, mentally, and emotionally as well as financially.

This lit a fire in me. I was angry about his absences, but his inconsistencies made me a more responsible parent. I take care of my kids in every way. They always know where I am, and if they need me, I'm just a phone call away. Some people's calls and text messages I respond slowly to, but if it's one of my kids, I'm going to respond.

My kids didn't ask to be in this world. I brought them here, so I'm responsible for them. My father taught me to be responsible in reverse. He wasn't there for me, so I am always there for my kids. I know what it's like to feel like my father didn't care for me, and I never want my kids to feel that way.

ALI

I decided to become a hustler at the age of fourteen, and the truth is, I've never stopped. I resigned from my position as a pharmaceutical street sales rep, but I'm still a hustler. I've switched teams, but I'm still in the game. My grind never stopped.

Even in prison, I was strategically planning my next move. Being locked up can really fuck with your mind. The key to protecting your mental health in prison is to never lose hope. You may be physically locked up, but if you keep your mind and your thoughts free, you'll be good.

I was in prison, but I was still hustling. Hustling is not just pushing a product or service; it's learning, growing, planning, gathering, and setting goals. I knew I wanted to be a full-time comedian, so it was the perfect time to polish my craft. I was around a bunch of bored, depressed muthafuckers who needed a good laugh. It was therapy for them and a growth opportunity for me.

I spent most of my time making them laugh and practicing my timing, delivery, and storytelling ability. I was also loading up on material because all kinds of crazy, newsworthy shit happens in prison. If I could comedically communicate those situations and scenarios to the free world, I'd be golden.

When I was released from prison, I was in the same position my mother was in at seventeen. All the odds were stacked against me, and I had to dig my way out of a hole. I was young, Black, poor, male, and a convicted felon.

The upside was, I walked out of prison with a plan. My plan had to work because it was literally all I had. If I wanted to have any kind of quality of life, I had to take it by force. Excuses, sob stories, and feeling sorry for myself were out the window.

Honestly, going to prison was my fault. I set that domino avalanche in motion. My mother had established a good life for her children. Selling drugs was a very poor personal choice that should not have been made. Now, I had to go for it. It was me against the world. I bet all the chips on myself, and I made it happen.

Two months after being released from prison, I was on a stage doing comedy. I used the finesse of my father and the fortitude of my mother to position myself strategically to win. I got a job at a men's clothing store so I could get discounts on suits for my shows. I didn't have a car, so I moved two blocks away from a comedy club that had an amateur night.

I put my name on the list every week until they gave me a chance. Once an opportunity presented itself, I took the stage and knocked it out of the park. Eventually, the club owner made me the host of the shows on Friday, Saturday, and Sunday nights. I also worked at a kiosk selling cell phone cases in the mall so I could invite people to the comedy club.

Hosting shows exposed me to many comedic legends, as well as legends in the making, like Steve Harvey, D. L. Hughley, Cedric the Entertainer, Bill Bellamy, etc. I intentionally established connections with them, and some of them helped take my comedy on the road.

I went from hosting to touring to television in a year's time. Being on the road helped me to become a better comedian. I learned how to flow with different crowds and audiences in different cities. Jokes that worked in Philly might not work in Atlanta, and vice versa. It was a learning curve that was included in the hustle, and I embraced it.

The ups, downs, and hardness of being on the road away from my family were all systematic. They worked together to help me achieve my goals. I wanted it. I dreamed about it. I hoped for it. I hustled to make it happen. Now it's a reality.

I don't complain. I just take it all in and roll with the punches. The dominos are falling, but this time in the right direction. Painting a picture of my life is what I always wanted.

The cool thing about hustling is that it pleases the Almighty because you are operating in faith. Faith requires work, and when you start moving toward your destiny and purpose, God will open doors in your life that you didn't know were possible.

Expert domino creators have these brilliant, beautiful effects that happen at certain times in their presentation that they know where and when they are supposed to happen. It's a part of the design, but the dominos have to be falling a certain way for the effect to happen.

God also hides blessings that can only be received when you are working, moving, and flowing in a positive direction. Brilliant, beautiful, and bountiful blessings happen when you position yourself properly. You can't get there with hope. The only way is through hustle.

I am grateful for the hustle. It has caused me to travel the world, permeate the air waves through radio and television, and most importantly, take care of my family.

When my father passed away, he was debt-free because I made that happen for him. I am able to take care of my mother, my wife, and all of my kids through one word…hustle. It's a code for me. It's what I live by, what I'll die by, and a principle I will pass on to my children. "Don't hope, *hustle*."

> *My father told me, "If you're already prepared for something, then where's the mistakes if you're already prepared?"*

Somewhere somebody has to
say something.
"Let's stop promoting the bad guy
in society as the top thing.
What's wrong with the good guy?...
Why does it have to be the bad guy?

I want to be big enough and
influential enough to say,
"Hey, this is what success is.
It's being happy all the time."

I want to convince everybody
they are able to change
what's going on in America."

"*...People in society need to stop making the mistake of thinking that you have time to wallow in something that happens to you.*"

Made in the USA
Middletown, DE
28 October 2023